From the first time I "met" Amber - Quotes cause we were online in the early days of COVID - we were on a podcast together .. I was immediately infected by her spirit and love. As a fellow walking wounded, I recognized her as tribe. *The Unrooted Bloom* and the way each page spoke to, as well as, into my soul is a journey of Black life, of half-breeds like me, from chapter one where she speaks courageous truths about those that birthed us into this world that many of us will choke on until we take our last breaths. Vulnerability, rage, sorrow jumps off the page as her pen pours out hope, bruising, fear and prayers for the men and children in our lives & she ends with where so many of us must (and cause we're Black - do) if we are to survive - self love, forgiveness and redemption. Brilliant work. Amazing Woman. Fierce warrior who fights for her people (and most importantly for herself) in the streets and on the page.

—Cat Brooks

THE UNROOTED BLOOM

The Unrooted Bloom

Amber Allen-Peirson
(Clarity)

BLACK LAWRENCE PRESS

Black
Lawrence
Press

www.blacklawrence.com

Executive Editor: Diane Goettel
Book and Cover Design: Zoe Norvell
Cover Artwork: "Graffiti Flower Root" by Tony Rubino

Published 2024 by Black Lawrence Press.
Printed in the United States.

I dedicate this to my greatest teacher, my son, Cordell Coleman.
Thank you for choosing me.
For all the people who taught me how to walk away.

CONTENTS

CHAPTER 4 — FIENDING

CHAPTER 5 — FAITH & REDEMPTION

Foreword

Amber Allen-Peirson's work, as you will soon discover, is astonishing, as brazenly truthful as one can be, and yet human, humble and even charming at the same time. I invite you to come enter the world Allen-Peirson has created, in which you will get to know a woman of extraordinary heart and talent, and, I believe, your own most authentic self.

The words she has chosen and arranged with which to tell her story and her family kept ambushing me with their brilliance and poignancy. Stories and memories, insights into one girl woman, into tough families and heartbreaking glorious humanity, are shared sometimes as prayers, and incantations; other times as plainsong, and quiet conversation.

These poems are about a biracial girl, with a white mother and black father, and enough pain between the two to light the whole neighborhood in Oakland. They are about neglect and spirit, abuse and the soul's victory garden, intergenerational chaos and grace, rage and redeeming love. They are a kind of owner's manual on channeling the radiant strength we find in accepting our deep vulnerability, our shot at lives of gratitude and wonder rather than of victimhood and defeat. They are about trying to navigate and heal from racism and misogyny, societal and paternal. They are about the birth of an artist from all this mess, the birth of a soul, the reality of great searing pain and resurrection, the path of transformation to a life of presence, power and humility, a life hugely lived equally in spirit and in service to the world.

I cannot say enough about *The Unrooted Bloom* and its author Amber Allen-Peirson. You hold in your hands a book full of truth and pleasure, mesmerizing, hypnotic and paradoxically, deeply human, a book grounded in the earth, that soars, like its author. All I can add is, Wow, and thank you.

—Anne Lamott

MATRIARCHS
&
PATRIARCHS

Rerooted

She is broken limb from family tree
    Rerooted
white bloom
stemmed from sick seed
      Sprouting
reaching
searching for
    Black root
        ginger
            &
           aloe vera

My Mother did not feel like
she belonged to her life
so she left it

Traded yellow stones for palm trees
packed her suitcase full of dreams
folded neatly
between a fat slice of humble pie
and her high definition rose colored glasses
Hung her childhood
with the skeletons in her closet
left legacies shattered beneath her bed
with the boogieman and rotten uncles
Washed away footprints in the sand

redirected bloodlines in her veins
Used her womb as a garden
planted Black babies with intention

She was alone
learning life's cold shoulder
turning cheeks and raising babies
with fathers that could not bear the weight
of loving her
they left

She was alone
unlearning the farm she left behind
concrete and coast lines
Brown babies on her white hips

She did her best

I am her fruit
the labor of her journey
Alone
She carried me
with what she had
Sprouted in the splintered places
She broke from

I Bloomed
I am her new seed in fresh soil
hybrid hope and lonely dreams
I am the first Spring of new thoughts

I am
The reason she chose to break free
I called HER
I honor HER
I am grateful she was brave enough
to make me
Her dreams actualized

My Body Still Remembers

My body still remembers
the resistance
the hesitation
I am skeptical of this world
      I was not sure
I wanted to be here
contractions tickled in my Mother's womb for 56 hours before they
cut her open
and pulled me out
      choking and blue

My body still remembers
how much I have always wanted to belong
to my Mother
to stay
      inside of her
where the idea of me was easier to love

I came into this world
isolated and incubated
quarantined from touch
and the body remembers
      being alone
without air in my lungs
or lips on my forehead

She could not hold me
welcome me to her flesh
        She could not nourish me
with nipple or kiss
and I cannot forget
        lonely
my old friend

Lonely looks like
hospital ceilings and fluorescent lights
through incubated plexiglass
Lonely sounds like
machines beeping
in an orchestra of crying brethren
Lonely feels like
tubes in my airways
and needles in my skin
        Lonely saved me

Three weeks later
She was wheeled to me in a chair
        eyes met me in my lonely

        She cannot see
the missed moments
        She cannot see
the way I have settled into my incubator
the way her body
        My home
        is unfamiliar

We lost more than umbilical cords
            Cut too soon

I am shaped by the lonely
that welcomed me to this world
and the body still remembers

My Mother's Eyes

       In my Mother's eyes
I am not an apple   I am
prickly pear
squeeze of lemon
salt and onion

       She cannot see me
past her uncried oceans
       She cannot see me
beyond her rose colored glasses
       She cannot see she
       She cannot see me

Trauma can be addicting
when it is all you know
Lives lived in normalized numbness
a tasteless tongue eating shit
pretending to love it

I keep trying to break her open
crack her code
create more than connected coping
with her
       I want to grieve
with her
       I want to rage

with her
        I want to heal
with her
        I want to laugh

        Let go

Open hands
        Free
Teach me how to pray
Teach me how to love with
open palms
        Holding air

In my Mother's eyes
        I am fire
Too big to fit in the space she made for me
Behind the books
above the cat food
next to the bust of Buddha

She wants me to be sparks and embers
        I am
roaring blue flames

I beg for kindle
She gives me water

        Scorch Earth

She did not know what to do with my fire
I burned
tumbleweeds and drybrush
arid lands
I am thirsty for her eyes to hold me like starlight
I want to see
a twinkle in her pupils and
see Myself

Cheek Bones

My Grandmother
left me in a life
with mirrors that only showed me
half of myself
      Split and broken

Where did my cheekbones come from

She
      rejected
the womb I was born in
wrapped in the White flesh of my Mother
the mistake of my father
I am the child of black sheep
placed under white wool rugs
      on both sides
My Grandmother wished there was more melanin in my Mother's
flesh
more sweet blackness in her blood
My Grandmother wished there was more melanin in her own sweet
milky Black body

We come in all shades and colors
We cannot pick our hue
That is God's work

She did not approve
of my daddy's choices
looked too much like the skin
She hated living in
            pale Black girl stuck in gray
learns to hate White
learns to hate my White Mother
does not look for me
in the life my Mother built for me to live in
with half stories and half mirrors
            Half breed
I wonder where she learned the rejection she offered me
            I did not fit the code
carried to California from Mississippi by way of Tennessee
Bougie Black

Brilliant
Bitter with reason

Sometimes
We do not know where to place it
Sometimes
We do not know who to give this hurt to

            She gave it to me
in cold shoulders and half empty mirrors
I never saw the hole
Never saw that I was half of a whole
too busy wondering

where my Black belongs
wondering why God picked this hue for me
did not know what to look for
till she came back for me
      Filled me
with ladies lunches
lists of beloved books
      with stories
of my lines drawn back
through American soil
Back to Mississippi
The place that tried to break US
      Connected
We did not break
      Connected
We did not break

My Grandmother's smile is like a mirror
We have matching cheekbones
and we hold stubborn truths
Her face shows me how I hold happiness
I become bee
      doting on her bloom
and She is perpetual spring to me now
I am learned tricks to her old dog
I am Black love in hues of creamy pink
I am visible veins in her Black blue blood
      I am healing in her harm
      We are perfect
      I am her cheekbones and legacy

Agape

Love
so many components
fitted like pieces of a puzzle
round edges and jagged corners
Holding each other

delicately clinging
like rose petals folded into their calyx
connected filaments
stemmed from empathy
rooted in forgiveness
grounded in compassion

It is the way a mother holds
her screaming child
"I love you anyways"
exhausted
with empty milk ducts
and broken eardrums
Unconditional

There are no absolute thresholds here
oxymora of loving a man who treats you with indifference
who treats life with indifference
The irony of bruises
pendulum swinging

seeking balance
        between you and me
                between me and me

We are only ever reflections of each other
I stare at my judgments like funhouse
        mirrors
unrecognizable parts of myself
Ponzo illusions of disconnection
between us
disoriented perceptions
I am the color of glass
with shades of my silhouette in your
        reflection

        Mother
I will always love you
in broken ways
It is how we were designed
Mosaic
Look at the sharp edges you gave me
Can you see them?
        I can

        Father
I cannot help but wish you knew the precious of little girls
Me
I wish I didn't know your fear so well
the way it slurs its words and curses cruelty in every direction
with fists and breath of smoke and fire

I wish someone taught you love
        I will

        To the Lovers
I have broken
caught between the sweet of my lips
and the sharp of my tongue
those scars were meant to be tattoos
Love bites
Do not forget how good burning feels
and healing
        I won't

        My Son
I am sorry
I should have known more things before I brought you here
Take it up with God
        I am

        Amber
        Thank you
For getting us this far

Wombman

There is a tunnel in
        My body
Light Guided Opening
Scripted with Glyphs
Translated to
Enter
        Welcome
        Life

Our beings
        The beginning
The entryway to breath
Containers of Creation
Architects of Existence
"There is nothing but mothers and our children on this Earth"
yet men posture themselves as gods

never learned to
        make offerings with seed for soil
never learned to
        harvest wombs and women
never learned to
        protect the bodies making babies

        In this lifetime
we are lost to the balance of our existence

the need to be in harmony with each other
        Interconnection
cannot untie the ties of life

I am affected by you
I am responsible for you

and yet babies are born
to Black Women in a world that steals the breath from our lungs
8 minutes and 46 seconds
traffic stops with broken tail lights
dreaming in bed
With lovers
lovers
lovers
lovers with fingers around the throats of Somebody's baby
Somebody's creator

We are unprotected
        making life in a world
that wages war on
        our bodies
and the
        Black Babies born from us
We are unprotected
in neighborhoods poisoned with lies that steal the love we whisper
to our children before dreaming
We are unprotected
sacrificing and pouring ourselves empty into our men begging for
return

Please
> Understand

Your worship of Me is not weakness

It is necessary

> Breathe
> Love
> Health
> Worth

Into Me

Into Us

Father

Lover

Brother

Son

Honor Me

> Honor Us
> Protect Me
> Protect Us

We are the portals to existence

You are the Givers of Life that We create

In Wombs that welcomed You here

> I honor You

Please return

Signed,

The Wombs of Black Women

Clarity

Snake skin uncoils flesh

> Unravel histories stains
> left in blood lines
> that create blood clots
> of separation between us

I got the house nigga blues
My blue eyes make you think I go the house
nigga views
My soul is a slave to the flesh of my master
and
You
can't see past the horizon to the Motherland
so you sit beneath foreign suns
ingesting foreign thoughts
institutionally poisoned and lost to
oppression

I was born to a Man
who connected to a Woman
in confusion and created
CLARITY

but you complicate my simplicities with
uneducated studies of Willie Lynch's

manuscript
I am not your enemy
I am nothing but your reflection
blue blood pumps in visible veins
while i search for self in vain
I took classes at Black bootcamp
strapped with glock 9's and defined as his
"down ass bitch"
which seemed to make sense
but my value
degraded by dollars and cents
I was losing my sense of self
while my people were gaining a sense of
stealth and shame
overcompensating for my other half

I wish I could shed shame

I wished I could dye my eyes brown and
inject more melanin in my flesh to prove to
you that I belong here
spoonfed me my identity
Mixed
with a little too much of this
and a little too much of that type thinking
girl get a perm before your hair gets to kinking

because you can pass

pass through life as a blank page

pass through youth in a blind rage
and pass by mirrors with a sense of self-hate
so deep because see
it is already 300 years of betrayal between us
yet we just met
and everytime I do something different from you
it brings skeptic wonder on my views of our history
so you reject
       the drum in my heartbeat
       the soul in my step
       the snap in my neck
leaving me
       to wish i was iridescent
I stand naked
       Praying for transparency
boil me down to the bone
and taste all my flavors
       I belong here
My Isness
Is the Isness of US

because Mama couldn't teach me to be who I am
all she could do was love me
as a reflection of her
and there is no rejection of her in my heart
She who taught me how to live life as an art
homemade values created from scratch
because I know her people never taught her no shit like that

I was born to a Woman

who connected to a Man
in confusion and created
CLARITY

but you complicate my simplicities
with uneducated studies of Tookie Williams' life
not all Black people carry guns
not all Black fathers abandon their sons
while you sit in the safety of your skin
watching too much CNN, Flavor of Love,
and Maury Povich paternity test another
father for that lost little girl
You think you know some shit
typecast my people as ignorant
because the stain of guilt left by our ancestors
is too much for you to clean up
so why try
instead you just get by
on society's cushion
      stuffed with cotton
            picked by my people
     plush
and the mention of racism is enough to make you blush
politically incorrect taboo
and you are to afraid
      to speak that much truth
           unless enraged

Loosen the noose on the tip of your tongue
because the truth is

We will never get past this place if we don't talk about it
and nobodies winning this race
so walk without your sense of caucacity
bring me blasphemy
and let's rip this shit open so it can properly heal

I will gladly speak to you about the Goddess in me
but check this shit out
I cannot be coined
no token tendencies
so we speak with a sense of sensitivity and compassion
I will attempt to minimize my knee jerk reactions
to your thoughts, questions, and comments
because I want to get past this place

I want to be fleshless
paint me purple
traversing between blues and reds
        Bloods and Crips
I cross color lines to civil wars
mediate between pores
and minimize the space between mine and yours
give me polkadots
let our souls connect like connect-o-dots
as we sit
        and simplify
                the complexity of complexions
                to Human

I was born to a Man and a Woman

Who connected in confusion
And created
CLARITY

Dear Daddy

Dear Daddy,
There Is
       a brokenness in me
passed down
from my Mother's shattered heart
I am shaped by the love
you never showed her
Her womb fed me the grief you gave her

      I am
the spit of your penis
the loin of your lust
the decision you never made

You were drowning in
White women
liquor
and cocaine
anything to ease the fear and the pain of being worthless
self pity over gratitude
fear of reaching
      your altitude
and being responsible
so you digress
You got a Master's degree
with no common sense

and there SHE was
sweet, loving, naive country bumpkin
now she's got your bun in her oven
What did you expect my Mother to do?
Exterminate my life?
        Vacuum my soul out, like old lint beneath the sofa?
Fuck that!

She hardly conceded
In fact, she carried on undefeated
determined to bless me with passion and nurture my dreams
love everlasting is what she showed me
while you hid
with your
bitterness
weakness
and fears
My umbilical cord fed me
        the taste of her tears

Nine months later I ripped through her body like Athena did Zeus
I came carrying
        compassion
        pain
        love
and my truth

On that day
I came to this Earth
as a broken hearted baby

You shoulda made different choices
Yours shoulda been
         one of the chorusing voices
that welcomed my life and the spirit in me
but you chose to go deeper into shame and misery
bitter
broken
blue eyed Black man
What is the story that made you imagine a world without our matching faces?
         I am a hall of your funhouse mirrors
Do you see yourself in my hurt?
Do you see yourself in my anger?
Where did you learn that type of resentment?
at the bottom of a bottle
or the end of a coke trail?
crack pipes and Newports

         I shoulda been enough
for you to mature in your life
live up to your potential
         and start to live right
My smile shoulda meant everything to you
but you couldn't even care for yourself
so with me you hardly knew what to do
         I grew
with the handicap of my broken heart
 never noticing the challenges that I faced from the start
"Daddy's little girl" didn't mean shit to me
 I had my Mother

my sister
my friends
and family
I was blessed

Until I met him

witty
smart
and ever so charming
Eyes that have never seen
noticed nothing alarming
in his age or occupation of street pharmacist
the type of nigga to avoid
is a class that I missed

I carried on
intrigued by the ways that he showed
me attention
what a real man should be had never been mentioned

My school counselor says I need to see things to keep the images in
my head
I am a visual learner
but you gave me nothing to see
which made it easy for this nigga to perpetrate me
He walked into my life
and took over my shine
He gave me everything a girl could want
I was wined and dined

diluted in the mind
played like a puppet
characterized with the doctrines of Disney and the Muppets
I wanted my Happily Ever After
but when the fuck did Prince Charming become such a fucking
bastard
      He broke me down
raised his voice and even higher his hand

but I thought I could be enough to change that boy into a man

      I shoulda been enough
for him to mature in his life
to live up to his potential
      and start to live right
My smile shoulda meant everything to him
but by now the light of my own self-worth began to dim
      I stayed on this path
continued to compromise myself
growing further and further from the feelings I felt
stunting my development and spreading thin just like jelly
until the swelling of life began to form in my belly

Umbilical cords filled with the tears of a baby born with a broken
heart
the legacy passed to a girl that never knew she was challenged from
the start
Because daddy you never picked me up when I fell
You never had a joke
a passage

or a story to tell
Never once did you ever cook me a meal
brush out my hair
or ask how I feel

You never spoke to me about men and boys
or attempted to guide me in my own growth
steer me clear from the noise

    You shoulda
sat on that couch with a shotgun when I went out on my first date
        made sure
he never kept me out too late
You shoulda made sure that he knew
that I was special to you

As a matter of fact fuck that
You shoulda
let me know too
You shoulda
beat up the first man
that ever broke my heart
but it was you!

My school counselor says I need to
see things to keep the images in my head
I am a student with no teacher
The only thing you taught me was how not
        to be enough

I Offer Forgiveness

I forgave him a long time ago
       accepted
who he is
brilliant alcoholic
watched his toxic life like a TV show on a channel I could not
change
       He would not listen
so I stopped talking
       He taught me
disappointment
desperation
and forgiveness

showed me the ugly of love when you live it fully
the way it can break skin and bruises souls without boundaries

       Boundaries and love belong together
they are symbiotic
interdependent identities
       We learned ourselves in this love we shaped with each other
this road we walked from nowhere to this place

This place
where little girls teach their fathers how to love them with what
they have
He had little

buried deep beneath the cast iron case of resentment he built
around himself
I had a shovel and some patience
I dug
There is treasure in toxic
when you're hell bent on looking
Lessons scripted in the invisible things he could not say

I learned a version of me in his eyes

I learned to earn the trust of a wounded beast
retracted teeth and claws
        I learned to teach
I learned what I look like
loved by an unloving man

To The Masculine

I am not sure what broke you
took
      wisdom
from your words
      humility
from your heart
replaced with vain and violent fear
      I am lost without you
navigating unjust juxtapositions

      searching
for your divinity in fistfights and orgasms
      screaming for God
either way

How did we get so lost from each other?
When did you stop recognizing me as you?

      I still see
the hues of your shadow in my reflection
      I know
you're somewhere quiet
In the place where prayers are just a conversation
just
      vibrations

Edges
Connected
    Belonging

I love you here always

In The Death Spiral

Dear God,

There is so much on my mind and heart that I feel crippled by overwhelm. I have not written to you in so long and I hope that you are not mad at me for staying away so long. I have not worked out. I have not been eating enough, drinking enough water, or meditating regularly. I am getting a lot done for Trap the Vote, mostly because my actions are guided by the loving men that I work with. I am struggling to maintain my work, and to be creative, or write.

My dad is dying. He was diagnosed with terminal lung cancer on October 16th and he has been wasting away for a while now and refusing to eat. He is at the end stage. In the process of getting his diagnoses there have been a lot of ups and downs, hope and grief, fear and acceptance. I have tried to be a loving daughter and care for him. He makes it so hard with his bite and venom. I need boundaries to protect myself which is hard to do when he is dying. Sometimes I wish I had more tolerance. Most of the time I wish he had more compassion. He lashed out at me last Friday for not taking him to a doctor's appointment that I told him two weeks earlier I couldn't take him to. I asked him to get us help. He has been sick every year for about 4 years in a row and he won't let too many people help but me. I can't, I don't have the capacity to do it all by myself. I am still dealing with Doodie too. I had to work and

I told him. It didn't matter at all and now he won't talk to me. I do not want my dad to die in a fight with me but I am afraid if I reach out he is going to lash out even more and I don't want that pain. I heard he is drinking and smoking again. I'm not sure if it's true. I know they have him on opioids. It sounds like he wants to fast track the process. I honor him and have no judgment of what he is choosing for himself. We all get to die how we want to. But what do I do? Try and force him to forgive me? Or let him be as he is?

I am sad and not surprised about his diagnosis and how he is handling it, including rejection and attacking me. It is his way. I am also angry. I am angry at the idea that our proximity and my bloodline obligates me to him and his care even though that was never true the other way around. I am angry at the disease of addiction, toxic parenting, Vietnam, lack of mental health services in the Black community, patriarchy, toxic masculinity, slavery, white people, Black people. I am angry at my dad for not nurturing me in a way that would have taught me how to nurture him now while he is dying. We are strangers in so many ways and there was never a chance for much more than I got. I also honor him in how he chooses to die, high and alone, bitter and afraid, privately with elements of grief, rage, and suicide.

It is strange to be so close to him and yet so far away from him. I will go through my daily actions and forget sometimes that my dad is dying a few apartments away from me. Other than the overgrown trees, I can see his front porch from my balcony. He is so close and yet I haven't seen him in a week. He is dying. I have thought about bringing him pineapple and just popping up but I am afraid he will be drunk. My dad is really mean and vicious when he is drunk. I don't think I have it in me to have my dying father attack me drunk. He has called so many people to tell them that I am a terrible daughter who abandoned him in his time of need because I missed his doctor's appointment. That hurts. They have subsequently called me to tell me they know that's not true and that I deserve peace. They have assured me he really actually loves me but he is lashing out in a grief-ridden death cry and that I do not have to reply. Sometimes I believe them and I am grateful for their comfort and assurance, sometimes I don't and my whole sense of self comes into question. Am I a good woman, good daughter, good person? Hospice is there to make him comfortable and I am also grateful for that. I do not know what I will be once my dad is not on this Earth. It seems that I will soon find out.

God please write to me through your pen.

Amber

Dear Amber,

Daughter you are mine and no one else's. You are loved, nurtured, and cared for by me indefinitely. Your father is human and he has bestowed you with many gifts in lessons of disappointment, anger, forgiveness, intelligence, and laughter. He has shown you your own strength and mind. Do not let the world set or limit your ideas and standards of love; you know better. You taught your father the love you know from me. You gifted him and healed yourself in your forgiveness of him and your love for yourself. I am proud of you and I will not abandon you when he dies. I will not abandon him either.

I am with him now in his pain, rage, and grief. His work is with me, not you.

But please, daughter write to me more often, drink water, and eat well. Get outside, exercise daily, and meditate actively every day. I cannot do those things for you but I have shown you that the discipline of these practices has powerful implications upon your life and spirit. Heal forever. You are carrying many wounds for yourself, your family, your community, and the world. That is how I designed you. Your empathy makes you sensitive and your vulnerability makes you powerful. The key to balancing those is self-care. You have to be the center of your own Universe in order to live in the frequency I designed for you. It is one of the hardest and most important things you can do.

You are exactly where you are supposed to be for now.

Trust and keep living in the love and faith that I have taught you, daughter. I am here and you are mine, always.

God

REST IN PEACE

KERRY ALAN PEIRSON

08/12/1948 - 12/30/2020

ESCAPISM

Boys To Men

This world wants us to birth broken men
snapped in pieces
circumcised sensitivity
lost lessons
stale bread crumbs to nowhere

Who can teach what you need to know?
Embody the gentle strength that belongs to you
Demystify stoicism and toxic masculinity
Imbue expression
True expression

        We crave you
folded into the sheets of our dreams
safely kissing peace in our bosoms
        We need you
armed with integrity and spirit
standing guard at the root of our Chakras

        Protecting

        We want you
giving life and love to this Earth
through our wombs and your character
pouring strength into beings
by being

by growing
by loving
by building
by creating
by protecting

With us

My Black Love

This heavy love
  thick and sweet
  slows time to an
       infinite endless

This
      heavy love
swells and wades in water
sediment and sage

This heavy love
center-point to unnamed constellations
navigates seasons and souls

This heavy love
weathered by chains and oceans
     carried on tongues
and tucked in traditions

    We
are heavy love
tattered tapestries and fraying fabric
mud cloth and kente
    griots
gripping gold
buried in the Atlantic Ocean

between docks and ports

We are heavy love
with this heavy love
watching
whispering
screaming
            carrying

            This heavy love
places candles in my window
and music in my soul

This heavy love is
            worth the weight
and I will carry it
            always

My Escape

I just want to
        feel something other than what I know
warm and fuzzy in the pit of my being
light and airy
from the souls of my feet to the curls on my head
I want to tingle in my womanhood
style myself each morning to catch your attention
dance through the day like a luna moth to your still night waters

I swear I smile more when you are around
I hardly know you
I hardly know two words to say together in your presence

Never saw myself as shy
I actually
        swallow butterflies
when you are around
My red undertone goes overtone
at the tender tone of your 'hellos'
        You make me blush
I like it

Crushed
sitting in between the words I cannot say
shy and smiling

I just want to feel something other than what I know
I do

Into The Constellations

I want to be loved
inside out
upside down
backside front
melting between time and space
as space dissolves like salt in water
        Between us

Blow me like hot soup
heat my hips into motions known to cause an ache in the belly
Bend my body into origami paper
place my kisses in a ziploc bag that can feed your appetite through-
out your day

I want to make orange with you
You can be red and I will be yellow
Blend like butter in my cream sauce
I want to taste all your flavors and feed you in courses
starting with dessert
Lick my sensitivities like ice cream
but no cherries on top
because you are dealing with a real Woman tonight
and I got this

It can be real easy for you
All you have to do is

        hand me your truth
and in return
        I will give you my trust
trust enough to take you to my secrets
show you how to push my buttons and what triggers can pluck my
string like a harp
let's make music

Introduce me to new
        octaves in my voice box
teach my tongue new forms of expression
and create cravings in my anatomy

        I see you
and I like what I see
so let me make this real clear
everything you have done before this moment is what got you here
everything you do from here on out is what will keep you here

My insides are
        connected to my outsides
        like roots are connected to trees
and the deeper you dig into my soils
the bigger your trunk will get
the tips of your branches will stretch past galaxies and into universes
I will upgrade you
by tomorrow life will feel lighter
I will help carry your load
and my love making will pump you up

like steroids
giving you strength
you never knew you had
You are my teacher
I am your tutor
so let us sit between the stars
and create equations

Instead I Find Bloody Love &
Broken Walls

Walls hold the rooms of houses
plaster and paint
stretched like skin over stud and bones
The living happens here
above floor boards
and between crown molding

There is a hole in the bedroom wall
where he rammed my head
broken and stained
too big to patch
I hid the cut and concussion
crouched on the floor of the closet
wishing I were invisible
just long enough for him to catch himself
breathing fire in my direction
Apologies taste like smoke rings and flowers

First taste of blood makes love look like bleeding
and he tells me that I am begging for it anyways
I believe him

My tongue is sharp
and maybe I shoulda known better

We thought we knew each other sacredly
because we had peeked past each other's flesh
to bones and blood
begging to crack me open
break me like eggshells
yoke our bruises into heart shapes to share
with each other on Valentine's Day

Twisted
      Knotty
            Messy
                  Sexy
                        Bloody
     Broken

but it was love

I forgive myself for living it so deeply

knife in hand
fist and teeth
grit and gunpowder

band-aids and ice
cotton swabs and rubbing alcohol
tears burn in fresh wounds
stitched and scarred

He looked like a broken mirror in the dark

distorted shadows

I became addicted to smoke rings
and flowers
to the upswing of his regret
We perpetrated each other in young ideas of possessive love
False power
Toxic coils of our darkest selves bound us
to each other in our shame

I could not have left a day before
I was ready
I could not have left without the people who patiently stood by and
waited for me
who held me broken
built me up
Let me grieve and process
the failing of my family
the fault lines in my foundation
Let me cry over my fallen house of cards

There are holes I will carry
in the walls of me forever
scars on my plaster and lies in my head of worthlessness and shame
Do not be a broken mirror in my darkness
Do not add negative cents to my empty piggy bank
Reflect me worthy
Hold me unconditionally
Give me a strong foundation to rebuild on

Love
stopped tasting like rusty blood in my mouth
my body stopped begging for bruises
and smoke rings make me nauseous
but there will always be scars

Hot Plates & Roses

The missing man
          I am looking for you
in the spaces between the stars
the holes of my whole
the silhouette of shadows
Your closeness smells of smoke and soot
          Your offerings
warm flames
lick my frozen places

I have lived on scorched Earth
          I have thirsted
tongue turned desert
dry branch and kindle
drought and doubt

I have used my palms
captured morning dew
turned ash and soil for till
watched the peek-a-boo of petals
          Pushing past
burnt oak trees and sycamore

Hot plates and roses
What do you do when all the flowers smell of fire and warning?
How do you remember Spring?

There is a season for burning
and
       a season for bloom

I am hungry for your seed
       I want
to give you this Earth I have made
       plant and harvest
I want to trust you with it
       cultivate crops of connection
clear the land
and control burn me back to life

I will try not to flinch
at your fist full of roses

Love Like Prayers

When you said you loved me
words like pin in a grenade
threat of explosion
      Be afraid
shrapnel & debris
collateral casualties and curled lips to show canines and claws
      I bite
I have needed to bite
beasts that tried to beat the bold from my bones

She is too important
to balance the fragile folds of empathies open
      I am open
lured in lion's den
I fought to be
      alone
Safe and alone

But you love me
like prayers and peace
five times daily

You love me
like listening ears
      collect me
eyes that memorize my mood and interpret my twitched muscles

You love me
        steady & patient
You love me when I push

Retract claws
No need for them here
I put my teeth away
        Now what?
        What does love look like?

Knowing

I gave our child your name
offered my tiny body to birth your seed
traded 206 bones to be your rib
You broke me
fractured then snapped
could not hold me delicate
leave room in your palm for my wings
Your fingers
cage around my throat
  Words
    Trapped
in straight jackets of circular behavior
You danced around my flame
I burned in effigy to our ideas of love
legs wrapped hard around your history
I tried to create your future
tried to be peace place of
change
the magic of erasures
cannot eliminate what the memories of our existence were designed
to be
  You
    Me
     We
were trying to fix what we did not understand
with fists and fire

We know now

Freedom

      Freedom
I gave it away before I knew what it was
No one taught me the precious of my body
No one taught me what it meant to give him my womb
a place to plant
tethered and tied by the umbilical of his penis spit
Seed in me

      Trapped
by hope
in all the ways I wish he knew how to tend the roots and till the
weeds
overgrown resentments
scorched Earth
We set fire to each other over and over again
trying to burn new things
trying to find freedom
trying to raise our SUN

What will grow here?
in this arid land
in this place of thorns and bruises

I hope
I pray
for
Freedom and forgiveness

BIRTHING

My Sun

      He was born
with chicken legs and chocolate drop eyes
fingers that had to learn to grip at my index
head like a potato

      My Sun
shifted the Earth off its axis
        For me

Young girl
20 rotations
watched my belly swell
held his heartbeat
contracted my life to him in each contraction

      I became a planet to my Sun
revolved completely around his existence
He was life's redemption
        Mine
in my mind
I could change the trajectory of the entire world by loving him

I could fix all my broken
heal all my hurt
and undue disappointment
He was swaddled in trauma's hope

breastfed unfair expectations

He was his father's unsaid apology
my father's unfelt love
His Mother's earnest dream
poor kid

My Heartbeat

He is seed and core to the apple in my eye
ground that holds my feet
sky that makes me wonder

THAT KID IS THE GREATEST GIFT MY LIFE HAS
GIVEN ME

Purest form of love I have ever known
my best reflection is my Motherhood
payoff in his smile
My pride is in his confidence
he is compassion in action everywhere he goes
I watch him exist the prayers I prayed to my womb
placed hope in my belly button
pushed him
shining light in a dark world
He does not have to be as amazing as he is
I would love him anyways
but he is
thoughtful and kind
witty and wise
confident
capable
creative
funny as hell

He is sunshine rising in my morning
the reason I reach to be bigger and better
in everything I do
My weakness and strength in one breath
I twist and turn in sleepless dreams of his future
wake to watch him navigate this life
like compass clocked
north bound
Rising starshine
     Hope
            Heartbeat bumps outside my chest
broken cage of my ribs for his sing song

HE IS THE BEST DECISION I EVER MADE

My Happy Place

All my homework is done
refrigerator is full
bills are paid
and there is money in my pocket
sunshine and time are on our side

Pick a place
any place
      I will take you there
baby boy
transmission light is not on in my car
      I trust it
to take us to the moon if you ask
I will pack sandwiches and water bottles
      Teach you
sing along songs
We can tell stories round-robin style
No TV or radio
laughter plays like soundtrack to our day
This is what makes Peter Pan fly

You Are Mama's Boy

Sometimes I wish I could ball you up and
stick you back into my womb
reconnect umbilical cords
grow skin as thick as leather
       to protect you
I would turn inside out to visit your smile
create playgrounds in my uterus
send my inner child to be your companion
       Here
            Safe
                In me
where I could swallow the stars to feed you bedtime stories
sing lullabies to the rhythm of MY heartbeat
filter my lungs to purify your every breath
I would spend a lifetime of stretched skin and swollen ankles
if only I knew
that it would protect you

from your daddy's selfishness
and your mommy's fears
from this confused world and the burdens it hands to you at birth
       Black boy's blues
I feel vulnerable
weak to the images you seek
I cannot be your flame sweet moth
 it is not natural

so empty inside
my skin still turns thick
and my heart sings to emptiness
holding on to nothing
as it slips between my fingers
desensitizing to how much
I cannot do for you
I hide my face from you in the shadows
hoping you don't see how
      Broken
I really am
      Broken
like the first promise

the first day
the first night
that I missed your bedtime story
catatonic
from five 10 hour shifts to make up where he left off
      Broken
like your first tickle me Elmo
smashed to bits against walls that seemed to change colors the
longer I stayed
      Broken
like syllables in words used for the
sole purpose of breaking me
      I am broken
because you cannot win

Double-edge swords slice you in half

and me in quarters
another fatherless child with a Mother
who was raised as a fatherless child
I cannot fix who your father is
I do not have the equipment to teach you
all you need to know
I am a caveman with a computer
Your eyes ask questions
I do not have the answers to
hands tied tight behind my back
I need him
but my need for him will poison you
if I let it

He cannot be what you see
eyes like sponges
I want to paint your picture
soak it into cells
recreate your DNA so there is no connection
I wish I knew
I wish I knew
I wish I knew how to make it easier
I wish I could blow a bubble big enough
for you to fit into
or create a body suit of cotton
wrap you up
and soften your truth
I know that I cannot ball you and stick you back into my womb
so
        this is my prayer for you my Sun

I do not want you to see another tear
       You
catch me crying
taste my tears
in the palm of your hands
thank you   you say
       thank you
You tell me my tears are like vitamins
nourishing your soul
and enlarging your spirit
       I listen
listen to what you tell me
singing songs in the rhythms of YOUR heartbeat
       You
laugh lovingly at my insecurities
You tell me my womb is too dark
for the light you have to share
You reconnect broken promises
You promise to find strength
in my weakness
and forgiveness in your daddy's choices
I listen
I listen to your eyes smile
I hear you tell your own story

Ancient Egyptian Hermetic Mathematics
1+1=2
two is a greater number than either one
       You

My Sun
are a two

You promise to do better
You promise to be better
than him or me
My humility becomes my greatest gift
        I will give you
every tear
every smile
every laugh
every shout
thin out my skin
let you see my fullest self
watch my fear become my courage
and my weaknesses become my strengths
        You inspire me

I will spend a lifetime of stretched heart space and swollen emo-
tions
all available to you
because I know you need no protection

You are safe
        in your own skin
                and in my love

Rising

They are precious
pressure & conflict
pressing heavy on the rough of the spirit

It is alchemy really
the way Black boys wake up in the morning
love like oil wells
deep drills and pipelines
You have to dig sometimes
the truth is buried in the memory of melanin
gift from the sun to our sons
the seed of our daughters

We may have forgotten
what it feels like to belong to the land where we live
Our history is triangulated in the Atlantic Ocean
the tomb of our treasures
rusted shackles and bone

I can see it
in the chocolate drop eyes of our children
the spin top energy of our boys
the strength and grace of our daughters

Do not measure me by the West of your world
We come from the center of existence

Recalibrate
My children are not defined by the choke hold of your traditions
Recalibrate
My men move like thunder and molasses
Recalibrate

     We are descendants of survivors and truth
cannot be buried in oceans or stolen soils
soaked in blood from noose to bullet
and yet we are here
pressure and conflict
the alchemy of morning
Rising

Pre-Teen

He is outgrowing the box I put him in
pries my fingers from the death grip I have on his existence
I know it is inevitable
I know it is healthy
My hands feel shipwrecked
when I am not holding him
heavy in my palms
I shift to lift him into himself
then fold
collapsed into
          Fear
This is where my logic coaches emotions
it is not fair
to fear the man he will become
because of the men I have known
Stop stacking bricks on his shoulders
breaking social role models of mom and man to be
let go of the bar I set above him
and let him be what the day calls of him
My work is not done here
it never will be
My loose hand swings in the open air
He takes it
He holds it
We keep moving forward

Tug-Of-War

I raised him
to wear his seatbelt in a car
look both ways before crossing the street
and not to take candy from strangers
epigynous of caution
Beware of the boogeyman
I raised him
in the kiss of my tickle monster
and the magic of crustless peanut butter and jelly sandwiches
with *Goodnight Moon* and Dr. Seuss before bed
He loved like popsicles in the summer
Or hide-and-seek at the park
Laughter
the soundtrack of his childhood
Why do we steal words from the tongues of our boys?
Trap them in the silent terror of hyper masculinity?
I did not raise him
to be entitled to the body of a woman
or to be afraid of his feelings
I am in a tug-of-war for the humanity of my son
with a culture that circumcises anything soft or tender from a boy's
being
I raised him to think
planted a garden of perspectives in his head
Please do not chop his blooms
allow him room to manifest the balance of his soul

No More Mama's Boy

My Motherhood is selfish
ego wrapped kisses
His existence
is attached to my sense of self
like roots to trees
I do not know
      who I would be
           without him
Lost without his look of security
when he sees me
His need
      feeds me
as if we are still attached
by reversed umbilical connections

I grow as mommy
defined by his bedtime
My list of dreams
transforms into his needs
      Life becomes vicarious
           or
      Not at all

He grows into unrecognizable mannerisms
Sigmund twitches in his grave
I know how to change diapers

read bedtime stories

       I am lost
on how to deal with
this little person
whose favorite subjects
are poop
candy
video games
His locker room discussions
are disrupting
MY maternity

This is when life becomes confusing
right about the moment
when I want to break up with my son
our interests are not the same
I do not know what my interests are
besides him
I am bitter with what is not natural
I am sure that this is all natural
except
       Right here
           Right now
where I wish
his daddy would step in and step up
Pray for us

More Than Necessary

       I cannot teach him
how to shave
pee standing up
or adjust his spirit in the body growing around him

The new octaves in his voice box
make him smile the way he used to
with a new toy in his hand
and girls
oh the girls
dancing around his head
like mothballs at a campfire
       Hormones are like opposite magnets pulling on each other

       My son is growing
into a distant dream
a thing I did once
or a person I used to know

There are crickets in his bedroom
and stains on my carpet from candy wrappers tucked behind my
sofa
it is quiet in the morning
without the buzzing of his alarm clock waking me to wake him

We talk on the phone

He gives me middle school colloquiums
I try to Mother from a distance
"Did you brush your teeth?"
"What did you have for lunch?"
"Are you getting enough sleep?"
              Me
poking holes
begging for a piece of his life
to keep in my pocket
tucked safely in the place where my ego
and Motherhood hold hands

He is happy
walking in the shadow
of his father's masculinity
I cannot teach him to be a man
I pray
His father can

It has been a long road
The 13 years we have walked as parents
enemies and friends
lovers from once upon a time
it is scary to be so vulnerable to him
I am walking the periphery of my life
looking in at the magic that happens when you face your worst fears
it ain't so scary
it's more than necessary

Black Mothers

I have had a visceral reaction to my son asking me if he can go and hang out with his friends ever since the Trayvon Martin verdict; gut clenching, cold sweating, short breathing, just plain old overwhelming reaction. Today is actually the first day that I have allowed him to participate in his regular romp and I have called or texted him every 30 to 45 minutes. Him and his friends are like something between *Huckleberry Finn* and the *Lord of the Flies*. Whenever they get a chance it is off on another adventure from crabbing in the creek, bike rides for miles, or scrounging their change together to make a movie. I have always been grateful for his core group of friends and the spirited, youthful way they all run together during the summer.

To me, adventure is what childhood is supposed to be about. You have to create a core foundation of joy and love for children to carry with them into adulthood. This freedom teaches them a sense of independence and confidence that one of my many long-winded lectures could never give him. It is the joy that trains them all into being real life soldiers. You have to have a sense of that kind of love and happiness to have something worth fighting for. However, ever since Saturday, July 13, 2013, when the Zimmerman verdict was announced, I have wanted to lock him up behind the walls of my house and find a Walmart to purchase every gun I can afford.

What is happening to me? How do I manage the fear that has crawled inside my being? It is beginning to fester. I am a logical person, with enough metacognition to know that it is irrational for me to raise my son from this place and yet it is not so irrational at all. I cannot stop imagining the empty hole in the lives of Tracy Martin, Sybrina Fulton, and everyone else who knew and loved Trayvon intimately. They have been so strong and graceful throughout this entire process but at the end of the day their son is not in his bed, or arguing over drinking juice from the carton, homework, curfew. He is not kissing his Mother and telling her he loves her or watching a game with his father, who adored him. They did not create his life in order for him to lose it as a martyr. He is gone and I cannot get past that reality enough to catch my breath when my son wants to resume his twelve-year-old life. My empathy as a Mother keeps me awake at night with the sound of skittles being chewed in my mind and the smell of wet concrete. I catch myself breathless when I think of what Trayvon felt the moment he noticed the shadow of Zimmerman lingering behind him in his ominous way. Did he wish that his Mother or father were there? Was he trying to be tough to impress Rachel on the other end of his phone? Was he scared? At this point I am crying again; sitting in Starbucks trying to hold back the overwhelming helplessness I feel at the thought of Trayvon alone and afraid in the dark when Zimmerman approached him.

I have to pause and call my son again. I need to hear his voice and reassure myself of his ever-important life. He is patient with me and understands my fear, sort of, or at least he indulges me. He was with me sobbing and heaving after seeing the movie *Fruitvale Station* about the death of Oscar Grant on Friday and again the next day when the verdict was announced. He cried too and hugged me without really understanding the full context of what was going on (though he understands a lot). He was more worried for me than for himself and he cannot understand how ironic that is.

I wish I had magic powers and I could fix the skewed cruelties that exist in human behavior. I wish I could bring Trayvon back to his parents and I wish I could assure my son's safety at all times; I cannot do any of those things and it is eating me alive. So the best I have got is to go to what I always have and write. I am going to use this space to unpack myself. Whatever I write here and however I share it; this is my prayer, this is my hope, and this is where I will heal parts of myself and anyone who participates in reading or dialoguing with me about what I share. Be gentle please. I feel fragile.

FIENDING

Contortion

It climbs inside your body
through any orifice open
         nostrils
                  throat
                           needle
injected in the skin
sucking souls between toes
         Smoke
blowing in the air

This demon diablo
indirect drive to death's door
after tortured morphs of the soul to unrecognizable souls

My son was only 15
when a friend shared his ritalin
wrapped in prescription bottle
that seemed safe encased in FDA approval
We trust doctors too much in this world
there is an oath after all

He thought it would help him concentrate
sharpened focus
for the excellent expectations
on Black boys
It is survival really

Trayvon Martin was killed 3 years earlier

       Drugs
freed my Sun from the fear of
being a Black boy
in a world that hates Black boys
I did not notice
too busy building a box of excellence and calling it home
I did not notice until my baby
was not in his body anymore

The Tenderloin is hell on Earth
a toxic place for tortured souls
trapped in narcotics kiss
held by the holy prayers of mothers
and grandmothers
bargaining with God for mercy
and redemption

       It will change you
snatch everything you thought you knew about yourself
contort convictions into manipulations
that only make sense
in the mad mind of a fiend

It is painful to watch
the wasting
the way he slips between my helpless hands

like

     sand

         water

             air

                 fire

Cannot hold his evaporating heartbeat

Recovery can only recover so much

Wandering Mother

More than once
       I have come to the edge of myself
          It is too much
peeked into oblivion
contemplated non-existence
felt the heavy of helplessness and the breaking of my own heart

More than once
I have witnessed my own expansion
learned my own resilience
and extended my edges
beyond what I thought I could

I can live broken
exist in the shadow of myself
hollow and empty
shattered hearts still beat

The alchemy of my fire
turned water
turned ice
tears hang like icicles on the sills of my eyelids
Waiting to thaw

My palms splayed
and open in the humility of vacant bedrooms and quiet nights

I do not trust my own words
they could betray the fragility of my existence
silence is the damn of my reservoir

Speak to me about anything besides the sadness that sits with me
at the dinner table
where he used to be

I have become an anchorless ship with nothing to land on
a wandering Mother whose knees are cracked and bleeding from
prayers

This is a new edge
one that I could not see coming
from horizons of any sunrise or sunset
one that makes the inflation of my lungs
a chore
This is a breaking of my broken
a plummeting of my pieces

Apparently
hearts turned to dust
still beat

In Muddy Grief

Progress interrupted
      it is hard to move forward
Grief is like mud
      My ankles are swallowed

Each step dirty and heavy

Visiting Day

Plate glass and telephones
My lips long to kiss your cheeks
     This place
dirty with heartbreak and shame
Names etched like tombstones in blue chipped paint
so-and-so was here
I won't put my name
neither will you

But we are here

Heavy

a thing seen
>> I can see the weight of myself
>>> in the eyes of the people who love me

>> Heavy

Alone

Infinite silence
No idea when the break will come
slice the lonely away
bitter eager and hopeful hesitation

Will you stay here?
How much should I open?
Make an altar for you to rest in
care in compensation
Do not leave me
Please

In this fun house
I do not recognize myself in the absence of mirrors
in the shapes of these shadows

Do you see me?
hiding in silence
       Alone
hoping to be seen

Coping

I sleep but do not dream
        I eat but cannot taste anything
I am tired of being numb

A Psychotic Break

Yesterday there was a crack in the universe
a whisper in his head
a dial in his pupils
I could see his edge like razor crossing wrists or throats
like hatchet hacking unnamed threat
        Suicide or homicide mind

How did we get here?
in the rubble of distortion
Can you see me?
Do you recognize the spot on my neck that twiddled you to dreams
as a baby?
My hands do not know where to be

Somebody help us please
Somebody tell me what to do
What sacrifices to make
What prayers to offer
How do I fight the invisible voices in his head?
How do I Mother from this place?

He is in a hell
I cannot go to
I tried
past my reach
        prayers stretch like fingertips

elastic snaps and so do people

He snaps
I stretch

Prius turns ambulance
Mother turns first responder

He is tucked in somebody's hospital begging for death

I am waking to the song of morning birds outside my window
making coffee
I have become good at trauma
practiced
I am not proud

I want to be good at something else

The Death Grip

Death grip
holding hope like breath
space
heavy hole and empty everything
exercised emotional muscle
worked in worry trying not to waste away

Faith
cries at night when nobodies looking
Faith
gets headaches and breaks out in hives
Faith
takes sea moss and vinegar in the morning
Faith
stretches to greet the sun
Faith
hurts

Stolen focus
I could not do a thing but hold space

He was here and we held him
breaking and dreaming
fighting and flailing

He is gone

again
We put him in God's hands
tucked in treatment
looking for his road to redemption

Fatigued in faith
I can let go
I can cry tonight
I can breathe
I can release this death grip
 and hold hope lightly

Cocooning

Backwards metamorphosis
butterfly
       cocooning
            into caterpillar

futile fetal
position

hibernating hermit crab
softshell

crawl back into skin
shallow breaths

until I am ready
to be deep

Legacies And Loss

No one knows what to say. No one knows how to comfort me in this cold reality. It is lonely, it is heavy, and sometimes I wonder if any of it is worth it. I am haunted, sitting on the floor of his empty bedroom, breathing in the dust, wondering if any of it ever settled on him while he was here.

Intimacy has always been a challenge for me. I was conditioned with romantic ideals of all relationships and how people are supposed to behave in them, which fostered many teachable moments of grief and disappointment. My Mother says, when I was a kid, I would yell at her about all the things she should have done, i.e. go to law school, marry a wealthy man, and get a little back bone before she had me so that I could be living the life I deserve. It hurt to watch her cope and fight instead of thriving in her life. I broke up with her, with friends, lovers, and family pretty regularly for not living up to my expectations (though I never actually strayed very far). Giving birth was supposed to make up for all that disappointment. The little life that I brought into this world, that I shaped and molded to fit my ideals of good and grace. He was the redemption of men who left my Mother, pimped my sister, and beat me. What a weight to be born into, it was too much to ask of anyone.

I was 18 when his father became my lover. Barely and freshly graduated from high school, I was cute, I was grown (in my own mind), and I wanted someone to save me from the dysfunction of my home and family. He spoke of love and made me laugh. I wanted to laugh.

I wanted to feel something besides the rage and grief I felt at my Mother's poor choices, something besides the fear and vulnerability.

My sister was 11 when she was kidnapped and turned out to heroine and prostitution. I was 14. My home was a kaleidoscope cage with shifting images of my Mother's tears, my sister's blood, and bruises across my pink flesh. I tried to protect them. I fought grown men who claimed rights over my sister's body with $100 hits on her head. As a kid, I had desperate and violent exchanges with women who tried to extract my baby sister from the palms of my prayer shaped fists desperate for favor with their pimps. I learned to live in the idea of fighting to the death, knowing the schismatic nature of escalation and conflict in my community could mean I might die or kill at any moment. I became a wildfire.

His father was only a few years older than me at 22 and he made me feel safe, at first. He was a Coleman, came from a tribe of mostly men, handsome, reckless, and deeply impacted by crack in the 80s. He was one of seven kids from a father who made a home out of five different women by planting babies in their bodies without knowing how to be emotionally responsible for any of them. He was wounded and so was I by these lives we were born into. We promised to be different, dreamt of dinner at the table and lawn mowers. My body stretched with our baby inside of me and we dared to dream of a peace and stability neither of us knew intimately.

We had never seen the love we wanted to be for each other, with no roadmap we became lost to our dreams and to each other. He was angry at his own life and I became the target of his projections and frustrations. My son watched his father put my head through a wall.

He saw me cry more than laugh. Our home became a kaleidoscope cage with shifting images of my blood and tears. I tried to protect him. He tried to protect me.

I left and the leaving is a story of its own but that is not what I am here for.

My son is now 19 years old, the age I was at his conception. He is beautiful, witty, smart, charming, and compassionate. He is also a heroin and meth addict living as a squatter in an abandoned church on Market Street in San Francisco. He is the oldest of five, on his father's side, and he spent his life watching me cope and fight while his father made a home from the bodies of five women who each made babies that he did not know how to be emotionally available for. These legacies are hard to break.

I am alone and tired of daring to love and giving myself away. I can't break up with my son and walk away as I have with relationships in the past. That is a part of my values. It is an invisible contract that I signed the moment he was being fed umbilically. I am in this, we are in this hell together and I am trying to find a way out for both of us.

I wonder what my son sees when he looks at me. What memories stand out in the fog of his brain. Is it the way I cut the edges off his peanut butter sandwiches after an afternoon at the park? Is it the books I read and the songs I sang to him at night before bed? Or is it the tears I cried for years and the wine I drank every night as he became a teenager trying to cope with the loneliness, over-whelm, and helplessness I felt? There were too many feelings to feel as he grew closer to his manhood. Before he ever touched a drug

I worried about my Black baby as I watched the world hate Black babies. I used to wonder if I had been stronger could I have saved him from ever engaging the vampiric nature of his addiction. If I had enrolled him in more programs, had more drug talks, or loved him harder would he have said no the first time a ritalin pill was offered to him at 15 years old? I wonder if my Mother felt the same way about my baby sister when she was in the streets. These legacies are hard to break.

It has been four years since the first time I found out my son was using drugs. There have been five treatment centers, the first one cost $20,000 and he left three weeks in after being committed on a 5150 for suicidal ideations. He was released with no plan for treatment, no resources, and no help. I dropped out of school to try and figure it out. I was in my first semester as a transfer student with a full scholarship to UC Berkeley.

I worked so hard to get into UC Berkeley and I have never made it back or finished my degree. Instead I have taken jobs for access to medical benefits that cover treatment centers. Spent hundreds of dollars driving to juvenile hall, jail, court, and treatment centers around the Bay Area. Started having uncontrollable panic attacks and spent time in a Kaiser intensive outpatient program. I have to save him. I would have slit my own wrists if I thought it would "save him" because he was the center of my world, the redemption of men who left my Mother, pimped my sister, and beat me. I wasn't sure I wanted to live without him anyways.

At first, it was easier not to speak to anyone about it and just silently witness myself in my broken world. Everyone had their own reaction to the news, shock, grief, anger but no one knew what to say. Sharing the reality of what was going on often meant I was left holding their feelings and my own. I stopped talking, stopped sharing, processing, crying, and grieving in the community. I buttoned up and hid behind cryptic Facebook messages and literary prose hidden deep in poetry's metaphor. It was lonely and hard but easier than trying to teach people what I did not know, which is how to support and love me through it. Grieving alone in despair was one of the most powerful, life changing, and enlightening things I have ever done. At first, I existed from sun up to sun down in constant pain, as if I was on fire. I burned and broke into someone unrecognizable to me. Old friends became strangers while new ones had no idea and I hid in high functionality and killer communication skills. You would've never known. Most people in my life had no idea because I gave no idea. I smiled, poured myself into other people's kids to compensate for the loss of my own. Offered, gave, cheered, showed up, and loved everybody with all I had, except myself, at first.

In the beginning I tried not to feel the emptiness. My alone time was spent binging on alcohol, sleep, and begging emotionally unavailable men to fix me. I do not judge myself for any of it. I was doing the best I could. It was unsustainable and at some point my sense of survival shifted to a new and sober model, thank God. There were many times that I thought I would die. There were many times I wanted to die because I thought the pain and fear was all I would ever be able to feel again. I was wrong, so very very wrong.

A part of me did die, the part of me that thought she was in control. Death to ideals, what I thought I knew as a 20-year-old girl giving birth to a life that I was never really in charge of. He was never mine and always mine and that is forever true. It is the somber, sobering place of loss. The dwelling of death and destruction, the humility of helplessness and it is a gift. Learning to hold things and people lightly with the freedom of faith has also taught me to value the people in my relationships as they are and not how I want them to be. It is more real and true than any ideals. My son is no longer living in my redemption, he is in his own. We will never be the same from here. We cannot go back. But we can go forward.

I am sitting on the balcony of my home writing; my son is in another treatment center that is covered by the benefits of a job I am grateful for. I am still hopeful for his recovery. I have learned to witness my own experience and hold dualities like unconditional love and boundaries, destruction and creativity, joy and grief all at the same time. I have learned to be still and steady when things are feverish and fluid. I have learned my own resilience.

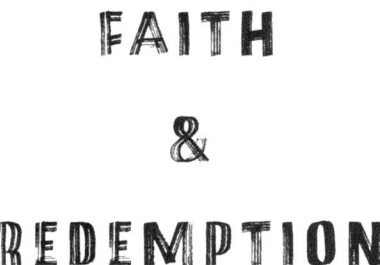

FAITH

&

REDEMPTION

Forgiveness

Forgiveness
is a conversation in the mirror
a guttural cry
burn ceremonies
sage smoke and salt
rice bowls

Forgiveness
is the shoreline
swallowed footsteps and sandcastles
it is a cleansing
a clearing
a washing

Unclenching of fists
to hold new things
like lovers around your fingers
or prayers in your palms

It is deep breath
        Release
        Relief
It is tree trunks bent towards the sun
It is the bloom of Spring after the death of Winter
a scar healed over
It is everywhere around us

Faith

It is hard to live in shadows
tucked in the intention of others
        Waiting
Paused
in your purpose
perpetrating small
It seems best for everyone else
Lies

        Breathe short breaths
even if you know you could swallow the ocean and spit it out clean
The world is on its knees begging you for you
but he matters most
        Values

I am humbled by the strength of my own soul
She impresses me
        Pressing on
with boulders on her shoulders
and rocks in her shoes
She keeps walking
        one step at a time

This is where real faith lives
on gurneys and hospital floors
        in clinics where doctors play God

in classrooms where teachers play Saints
in bedrooms with broken lovers and wine

I know my own divinity
I know His too
touched with creativity by the creator
I hold my breath with bleeding feet
Knowing
This too shall pass

Resilience

        Walk me through
life's dark maze
haunted halls
fears lurking around every corner
        abandoned
                rejected
                        taken for granted

        Hold my hand
whisper me focused
eyes adjusting to open
        Hoping
        you can forgive me for ever being born into this life I live
        it has become my darkest nightmare

My life might be too heavy to be loved in
What past life discretion earned me this karma?
I want to wipe my life away
        Clean slate
Abandon my loved ones to their choices
I am too afraid of being all alone
I sit centerpiece to dark circus chaos
        Clinging
to familiar family foe
tattoo my voice box "It is gonna be ok"
people search and seek to read me

tender tissue to YOUR tears

Who holds me?
chip away my shoulder
      I cannot be everyone's rock
solid soul of divine maker
I have proved my strength to myself
survivor of life's assaults

      I just want to flow in the direction of my favors
Stop swimming upstream

Enmeshed

I draw strength from his state of mind
symbiotic simpatico
We have always been close
touchstones tethered by invisible umbilical cords
strums and string
The music of mothers and sons

He hurts I hurt
I hurt He hurts

Self-care is how I love him for now
Hopefully soon
He can return the favor

Meanwhile

Fault lines
lay like nerves in earth
quake connections
surrounded by suicides
the kids are not ok

My hands are not cups
holding your half full
pouring all of me into your empty
I restore what has been given
I grieve what has been lost
a lifetime
a dream I bled for
a mirror I recognized

     Gone
Who am I without him?
Who am I in this limbo?
this hell between crib and casket

     Hands gripping air
holding hope like breath
He is somewhere in San Francisco
right across the bridge
$7 away
and yet I cannot reach him

cannot hold him and heal this harm

     It is God's work
Words of a helpless Mother whose hands are gripping air
meanwhile
I am in love
meanwhile
I have a job
meanwhile
February takes a leap and becomes March

I Am Learning To Release

My lower spine is degenerating
cannot support the weight of the world on my shoulders
I have to put some people down
make room for
　　　　joy in my life
cut cords to babies I did not birth
cold shoulder communities
practice "No"
Sit with my grief
bloody knees and salty cheeks

　　　Silence has loved me
kissed me in nightmare screaming and hopeless
I begged for noise but she did not come
I finally learned to hear the sound of my own thoughts
They are beautiful
like sunlit rivers
rapid
like the iridescent wings of a hummingbird
I pick up the scattered pieces of the puzzle
I call myself
put me back together
Let us see what I look like

A Letter To My Younger Self

There are no monsters under the bed
but be careful of the ones with charming smiles who don't wear
condoms

You were always enough
baked to perfection by the kiss of the sun
No one needs to tell you that for it to be true
Not your Mama
            Not your Daddy
                        No one

Take your time and focus on your development
Do not give yourself away
or you will not have anything left when the pandemic hits
            Focus

You have anxiety
take care of it
practice peace and breathing
learn to look at what you want to see
protect your precious

You will have to let him go
and there is nothing you can do about it

Stay sober

be gentle with yourself
get up and do something
anything

I hope to see you on the other side of this

Soul Searching

I am somewhere in between
pitched night & sunshine
screaming silence
violent peace
bitter sweet
still storm

Swinging dizzy

Bipolar pendulum of my life
grateful for my greatness
I resent the responsibility of my own thoughts
No blind bliss
I know too much
and never enough

Unkempt keeper
skeptical believer
giver who cannot receive
until depleted
            and
on my knees

The way I love scares me
  tipping scales
  desperate for balance

sit in solace and solitude
reflecting lessons of life
chisel away at confusion
till I find
Clarity

Earth Angels

Sometimes dreams and goals juxtapose into carbon monoxide
as necessary as breathing
One foot in front of the other
Reach in any direction to grab a handful of anything
       that means something
I want to glow
like Sirius star
Shine bright
      Alone
Constellations paint pictures in the sky
Collective
illustrations of time or timeless

My tongue paints Picassos
I fall like screw into groove
      Connected
like the invisible lines of Orion's belt
wrapped around the waist of time

This place has been good to me
Here
      I showed up
eyes closed
      heart open
         one foot in front of the other

This place
        Held
my hand through
first steps

Thank you

Ascent

I rise with the sun
and shine
shadow my past
reach for my future
hold the presence of my present
close to my chest

I am grateful
for deep breath moments
walking slumber
One foot in front of the other
I will get there one day
on road less traveled
full scale happy
Master of my own ambitions

I write to heal
I want to redesign the constellations
plant oak trees
ornamented in honey hives
stripped armor
down to my open
Redirect the circuits of my connections
I am wired
on sunshine
spring breezes

kissed by the song of birds

I nest
hatched from pain
and take flight

Family Counseling

Today was important. My Sun is still fighting for his life in treatment

His father and I joined three other families in an all-day Zoom meeting about the disease of addiction. We have done this before but not like this. It feels like this is really happening.

I have built walls between me and hope. I didn't realize it until the walls started crumbling.

I am open and it is scary.

Hope looks like scars left from hot plates that I have touched too many times. But this feels different. I am almost two years sober myself. I like this place. I have learned to feel new things

I have said unsaid things and I can hear the whole of a person in this place

Hope is heavy. I will hold it. I am tired.

I will rest and resurface tomorrow.

Leads To Anxiety

Cold stone slows my blood
heartbeats at the pace of hummingbird wings
          Anxiety is real
and I trust her in my body
She never lets me stray too far from self

She reminds me when I am empty
brings me back to center
Anxiety lives at the edge of me
Every time I come to the edge of myself and try to cross
She flutters my heartbeat
skin sticky with sweat
shallow breath and light blood

It is cold stone and water that brings me back
sits me in my center
reminds me where I belong
crossed leg with mudra hands
          Open heart

Keep going Amber

Marbles & Muscles

I have lost my mind a bit
somewhere between here and there
it slipped into a top hat and disappeared
There was nothing I could do
       It had to go
could not hold the hurt and the heavy
I understand
my mind and my marbles
       Weak
links in the chain
fragile pieces of me
       Gone

Everything that remains has muscle and teeth
wisdom and vim
vetted by heartbreak and brimstone

This is where new minds begin to build

Self-Love

There is a new hum when the crickets sing
a lukewarm wash away of the day
a peace in the quiet of my own thoughts
My words are unpacking candles and lavender oil
Take Five and Coltrane play
Soundtrack to my twilight

        There she is
that girl with fire in her stare and love on her tongue
unburied bits and pieces of her being
She will be stitched anew
I cannot wait to meet her again

Sober

Sitting in the power of my own being
choosing channeled choices
learned on the back end of drunk dials
     and walks of shame
black outs
     and toilet bowls
Anything
     not to feel nothing no more

I forgive you Amber

I can sit with it all now
     Hold myself
closely
in sober spirit
With mirrors in every direction
     Selah
         I see
the reason bottles seemed to be the answer
lost things and people
misplaced passions
The clashings of mind and soul
     acceptance and expectations
         grief and disappointment
     Boundaries
buried by blame and base perceptions of self

Give it to God

Dried out
climbed out from wishing wells
to work for clarity
        This place
like crystals
        Clear
ringing with God's grace
in the place where everything felt like too much
        Serenity
saved me
        Courage
changed me
        Wisdom
shaped me

Ase'
Amen
And so it is

Spirits

Oracle cards and candles
Sun salutations
Water
Breath
Rivers and oceans
Light between the leaves of redwood trees
The smell of bay leaves
Selah
Propagated ivy and sage
Tarot on new moons
The laughter of children
Hugs
Psilocybin under desert skies
Pulsing stars and sacred matrix from Sirius point
Tobacco and cacao
Rose water
White lotus
Tea leaves
Stoking fires
River rinse
          and
Salt soaks
Wash me over
Anointed
Rosehip and lavender
Shea moisture

Coconut water
Naps
Dreams
      and
Poetry

Humbled

It is a practice
learning the stillness of self
the soft underbelly of my strength
Solid
in silk and satin

I do not always have to be sharp and pointed
surrounded by insatiable connections
Thank you to life
for all the giving you have given me
all the abundance and beauty of breaking and building
the love of giving
the learning in receiving

I am humbled by small things
like invitations and blooming flowers
What is life?
but a string of moments
upward spiral in amniotic existence
moving from one point to the next
Birthing
new things pulled from everything
that already exists
particles and atoms
pushing and pulling
The opportunity of morning

reflection of evenings
New days turning under the cycle of the sun

Today
I bathed in sound
then soaked in the sun
thinking of how welcoming smiling eyes
can be
when speaking scary things
like love or desire

Forming friendships from places healed
Intention
to tend the weeds of abandonments roots so sunflowers can bloom
We can bond in the power of the things
we know
even when we forget

how much we are loved by God
or
the way the Universe bends in our favor
when we practice
the stillness of ourselves
speak beautiful things
from the belly of our beings
Into the truth of it all

In My Body

This morning I woke up
     in my body
Rose to the sunrise and praised
prayers and salutations
The day has been about sweet things
strawberries
tender talks that happen
between aunties and nieces

I checked a few boxes
got some things done
but mostly relished in the reflection
of my own recovery

     I am getting better and better
at this being Amber thing
at the focused love and healing
I give and get
at the expectation of peace
in my home
in my body
at the boundaries
at the asking
at the receiving
at the deserving
at the giving from overflow

at abundance

I would have lingered for months
lost in trauma a few years ago
I would have swam in the heavy of heartbreak
holding breath and dying
My turnaround was one day
Flat
with breath
          and prayer
saturated with what is not mine to hold
          Released

Today I woke up

completely in my body
with the ability to feel all my blessings
the bounty of my own existence
The love
          all around me
                    in me

These things can hide from view if you are not careful about what
you look at
          Perspective is a choice
and a powerful tool of faith and fortune
The ability to swing the things you see
sits inside the place of stillness
          You create
in the belly of your being

Practice and intention

This is what I learned today
when I woke up in my body

Home

Treat my front door as an altar
       My body
as a temple
        Place offerings
to ask for entrance

This is sacred ground
       Home
the quiet place
I hide to harvest everything
       Holy in me
Sacred healing happens here
selenite in every corner
scented with clary sage and lemongrass

     This is where I breathe
air filtered by
       prayer plants
           dumb cane
              and snake bush

This is where I use my hands to harvest
       Jalapenos

          Kale

             Lemons

and tomatoes

I eat here   in my home
Sleep
in a bed made of my favorite feels
I built an altar for warriors
a place to recoup what has been lost in war
Treat my goose down like holy water
        Baptized
in my body
this home
        has held me

There are things
Only me
God
and the flies on the wall
can speak about
what use to be
ghosts in picture frames
there are empty tables in this home
this shrine of my design
this is not a place for war and wounds
this is a place for laughter
for love and love making

Place your offering at my door

One Step At A Time

When this is done
I will quiet myself
silent retreat
to retrieve all that's been given
The too much
      and not enough
           of all the words

I hope to offer things with meaning
      I hope to receive
lessons of meaning in the offerings
      I give and
thicken my thin at the altar of myself
      ask you to witness
           my metamorphosis
This is a Phoenix fluttering
      in ash
           from fire

Everything I thought I knew has burned
the cradle is empty
      the urn of my father is with a candle at my altar

      To mother
           is to sit between the bookends
           of life and death

I am a created creator
humbled Goddess
Queen at my throne

A moment
        a day
                out of a life lived
Till death

Keep perspective Amber

Veins Reveal

Mama says
        Love
is like chewing glass
and we pray to the cuts in our mouth
drinking saltwater and lemonade
sacrificing ourselves to our egos

Daddy says
        We pray to fire
burning everything
like Earth and bridges
Fuck it all
I do not like the taste of blood in my mouth
I do not want to be swallowed by anger
        I am learning
olive branches
        Breathing
where screams use to be
The alchemy of lonely to sacred solitude
        Fists opened
so palms can hold the things meant for me
like laughter and dancing

Akashic records say
I belong to the blood in my body
mapped in

Veins
    that track like rivers
    In the Earth of me
I am whole and holy
I give from overflow and
fill my cup
        with things whispered to me by angels and ancestors in my
        sleep

I am the ember of what will burn
I am the giver of my daddy's grace and the recovery of my Mother's
tongue
I am the keeper of my own sacred self

Ase'
Amen
And so it is

The Miracle Of Me

The way my eyes see the colors of love
hiding in dark places
guttural laughter glows like gold
at the end of my rainbow
maps holding high roads
begging for my footprints

These lessons
insist on being learned
       Mastered
              Integrated
                    Shared

It is the way words and wisdom
marry in my mind
       my gift to give is
             clarity in confusion

Uncoil conditioning
from caregivers with no capacity
for heat
or the heavy of me
       Muscle
made from the weight

vetted

      Values
tested
      Tenacity
I have held loss
like heirloom of my ancestors
      Explored
deepened detachments
Healed disappointments
and bitter burns

Nothing is what I thought it would be
but everything is so beautiful

The budding of things learned on the other side of death and
  destruction
The excavation of iterations
incinerated waste
      Layered
in a life of legacy and loss

      I found
Precious in the pressure
         Power in the practice of
            Peace and prayer

My life is an offering
laid at the feet of seven generations

Photo: Stephanie Mohan

AMBER ALLEN-PEIRSON, aka Clarity is a powerful, empathic poet, activist, educator, orator, and consultant focused on being a catalyst for self-development and healing. She weaves her lived experiences, emotions and stories into literal metaphors, provoking reflection and visceral sensations in listeners. The process of writing is profoundly spiritual, like prayer for Amber. What she produces is a treat for human consumption. Amber coaches people and communities into seeking justice, achieving dreams, healing wounds, repairing relationships, and building stronger identities. Born and raised in Oakland, CA, she raised her son in the Bay Area where she still resides.